Slimy Sliders

Lynn Huggins-Cooper

QED Publishing

Copyright © QED Publishing 2008

First published in the UK in 2008 by
QED Publishing
A Quarto Group company
226 City Road
London EC1V 2TT
www.qed-publishing.co.uk

A catalogue record for this book is available from the
British Library.

ISBN 978 1 84835 053 3

Author: Lynn Huggins-Cooper
Edited, designed and picture researched by:
  Starry Dog Books Ltd
Consultant: Sally Morgan

Publisher: Steve Evans
Creative Director: Zeta Davies
Senior Editor: Amanda Askew

Picture credits
Key: t = top, b = bottom, l = left, r = right, c = centre,
FC = front cover, BC = back cover.

A = Alamy, BSP = Bigstockphoto.com, C = Corbis,
D = Dreamstime.com, DK = dkimages.com, F = Fotolibra,
G = Getty Images, ISP = iStockphoto.com, M = Morguefile.com,
NPL = Nature Picture Library, P= Photolibrary, PS = Photoshot,
S = Shutterstock.com, SDB = Starry Dog Books, SPL = Science
Photo Library.

1 S/ © clearviewstock; 2–3 M/ © Pickle; 4t ISP/ © Viorika
Prikhodko, 4b C/ © Otto Rogge; 5 C/ © Stuart Westmorland;
6t S/ © Steve McWilliam, 6b S/ © clearviewstock; 7 SPL/ Nigel
Cattlin/ Holt Studios International; 8t BSP/ © Greg Banks, 8b
A/ © B. G. Wilson Wildlife; 9 S/ © Milos Luzanin; 10t NPL/
© Rod Clarke/ John Downer Productions, 10–11 DK/ Frank
Greenaway © Dorling Kindersley; 11 C/ © DK Limited; 12t
G/ © Brian J Skerry, 12b PS/ © Roy Waller/NHPA; 13 C / ©
Stuart Westmorland; 14t D/ © Pufferfishy, 14b G/ © Stuart
Westmorland; 15 G/ © Roger Horrocks; 16t S/ © Troy
Casswell, 16–17 G/ © Gerry Ellis; 17 A/ © blickwinkel; 18bl ©
George Africa, 18bl (inset) D/ © Tonybaggett, 18–19t C/ ©
Michael & Patricia Fogden, 18–19b C/ © Michael & Patricia
Fogden; 20t SPL/ Philippe Psaila, 20b C/ © Joe McDonald; 21
C/ © Michael & Patricia Fogden; 22t C/ © Brandon D. Cole,
22b C/ © Chris Mattison; Frank Lane Picture Agency; 23
SPL/ Claude Nuridsany & Marie Perennou; 24t S/ © Thomas
Mounsey, 24b A/ © Holt Studios International Ltd; 25 A/
© blickwinkel; 26t S/ © Steve McWilliam, 26b PS/ © Daniel
Heuclin/NHPA; 27 C/ © Brandon D. Cole; 28t SDB/ © Nick
Lettett, 28bl SDB/ © Nick Leggett, 28br D/ © Klikk and
Robeo; 29 (main image) Beth Fisher, Cambridge Hands-On
Science (CHaOS) and S/ © Novikov Alex.

Contents

Slippery living

Slimy creatures often make people shudder. But slime comes in very useful for lots of animals. They may use it to help them move, to keep cool and damp, as a defence against **predators** or to protect their eggs.

▼ *In dry weather, the Australian burrowing frog burrows into the ground and makes itself a slimy **cocoon**. The slime keeps the frog moist. When it rains, the frog climbs out of its burrow.*

▲ *Earthworms produce slime that coats their bodies and helps them to slip through the soil.*

Slime for slipping along

Slime makes it easier for many animals to slip across surfaces or to burrow underground. Some creatures that do not have legs produce slime to help them slide quickly.

Other uses of slime

Some frogs and toads that live in dry, hot places ooze a slimy coating to keep themselves damp during dry periods. A number of salamander **species** produce poisonous slime to stop other creatures from eating them. Some snakes and lizards even use slimy **spittle** to help them to feed. They coat their **prey** in spit to help them swallow. Most **amphibians** lay eggs in water, inside a layer of slimy jelly. The jelly swells in the water and protects the young from cold, diseases and small predators.

Slimy fish

Fish produce slime from **cells** in the outside layer of their skin. The slime prevents many **parasites** from attaching themselves to the scales of the fish. The slime also provides a protective coat over wounds.

▲ *When parrotfish sleep, they cover themselves in a cocoon of slime to stop predators from sniffing them out.*

Sticky slugs

Slug slime helps prevent slugs from drying out. It also makes travelling across the ground easier and allows slugs to stick to steep surfaces. The slime from one slug even makes predators' tongues go numb, which protects the slug from attack.

▲ *The black slug covers itself in a thick foul-tasting mucus which protects it against predators and keeps it moist.*

▼ *Leopard slug slime, like the slime of other slugs, becomes more sticky if it gets wet, so it is better to rub off the slime rather than to try and wash it off.*

Black slug

The black slug can come in a variety of different colours, including brown and white. It is often active in the daytime, when other slugs are hiding from the sun under rocks and leaves. Gardeners see more of this slug than other slugs and tend to think it does more damage than other species. However, the black slug mainly eats dead and rotting plants.

Leopard slug

The leopard slug is common in Great Britain and Ireland. It now also lives along the east and west coasts of North America, which it reached by crawling ashore from European ships that travelled there. The leopard slug is well **camouflaged** with spots and stripes. It can grow up to 20 centimetres long – the length of a man's hand.

Slugs and snails are gastropods, which means 'stomach foot'. They move along on a single, squashy foot.

Grey field slug

The grey field slug is fairly small, at just 3 centimetres long, but is one of the most serious slug pests. It spends its life above ground feeding on plants, unlike most slugs, which spend most of their time in the earth. Like other slugs, it eats twice its body weight every day. It also breeds quickly, particularly when the weather is warm and damp.

▶ *The grey field slug can munch its way through whole fields of crops. Its slime is usually clear, but when the slug is disturbed the slime becomes thick, white and sticky.*

Slimy snails

Snails are found all over the world, in gardens, ponds, on the seashore, in the woods – everywhere! Their shells give them protection from predators and the drying effects of the wind and sun.

▼ *A baboon inspects a giant African land snail. The largest giant African land snail ever found was 37.5 centimetres long and weighed nearly 2 kilograms.*

▶ *Periwinkles are a favourite food of many seabirds. Some people also like to eat them, as the snails are high in **protein** and low in fat.*

Periwinkles

Periwinkles are snails that live on the seashore. At low tide the periwinkle is exposed to the air. To stop itself from drying out, it uses slime to seal the gap between its shell and the plant or rock it is on. This allows it to stay moist until the sea covers it again.

Giant African land snails

There are three species of giant African land snail. They are found in many warm, **tropical** countries. One species, the East African land snail, lives in Kenya and Tanzania, but is also found in south and east Asia, the Caribbean and many Pacific islands. It eats rotting plants, fruit and vegetables, as well as bones and shells that provide **calcium** to make its own shell strong.

Brown garden snail

The brown garden snail is common in Britain and Europe. It is found in gardens, parks, forests and even sand dunes. It feeds on rotting plants, **algae**, **fungi** and **lichen**. It is most active in wet weather and at night. If the weather gets too dry, the snail goes into its shell and seals the entrance. It can survive like this for months without water.

▶ *The brown garden snail has a long tongue, called a **radula**, covered in horny teeth. It eats by scraping the radula over food, such as lichen.*

Wriggly worms

Have you ever held a worm? If you have, you'll know exactly how slimy these wriggly creatures can be. Worms do not just live in soil. They also live in the sea and along the shoreline.

▲ *The velvet worm squirts slime at predators in self-defence as well as to catch prey.*

Velvet worms

Velvet worms live in **leaf litter** and rotten logs. They can capture animals, such as spiders, that are several times their own size. To do this, the velvet worm squirts sticky slime at its prey. The prey gets tangled in the slime and is unable to escape. The velvet worm then bites off parts of the captured animal and dribbles acid **saliva** on the parts to make them mushy. It then sucks the mush up into its mouth.

Ragworms

Ragworms are marine worms, which means they live in the sea. They build U- or J-shaped burrows in the sand or mud. The burrows are generally about 20 to 40 centimetres long. The ragworm spins a sticky 'web' across its burrow to catch tiny floating plants called **phytoplankton** from the water. It then eats the web and anything caught in it.

Parchment worm

The parchment worm lives on the coast of Britain in a tube that it **secretes** in the sand. Its body has three parts. The front part contains **glands** that secrete the tube it lives in. The middle part has winglike lobes that secrete the **mucus** that it uses to catch food particles from the water. The last part of its body is made up of lots of small segments.

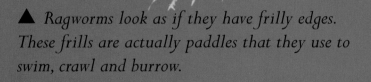

▲ Ragworms look as if they have frilly edges. These frills are actually paddles that they use to swim, crawl and burrow.

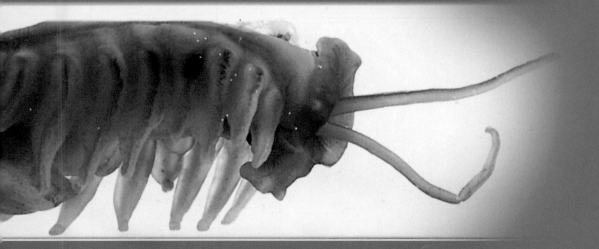

◄ The parchment worm gives off a gentle glow, particularly from its tail end. The glow may encourage predators to grasp its tail end rather than its head.

Slippery at sea

The sea has a huge variety of slimy, slippery beasts hidden in its depths. One of them, the giant squid, is as large as a sailing yacht. You wouldn't want to get wrapped up in its long, slimy **tentacles**!

◀ *Not many creatures are big enough to hunt the giant squid, but sperm whales and sleeper sharks will attack them.*

Giant squid

Giant squid live in deep water in all of the world's oceans, but they are rare in tropical and polar areas. They grow to huge sizes. Females can be up to 13 metres long and males up to 10 metres long, making them one of the biggest slimy creatures alive.

▼ *The sea hare's skin contains a slimy poison that makes it a nasty meal for predators.*

Sea hares

Sea hares are large, slimy sea slugs. They only eat plants that are the same colour as themselves. Sea hares use their colour for camouflage, hiding in seaweed. When scared, a sea hare squirts out ink to confuse predators, such as sea anemones.

Starfish

Starfish are found in all of the Earth's oceans. Scientists have been collecting starfish slime because they have found that it contains a material that may be useful in treating **allergies**, such as hay fever.

▼ *Many starfish eat clams and oysters. To get at the creature inside the shell, the starfish has to prise the two parts of the shell apart using the suckers on its arms.*

Foul fact!

A starfish has two stomachs. To help it digest food, it can push one stomach out through its mouth.

Squishy sea life

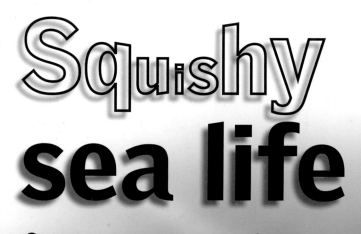

Some sea creatures have very soft bodies. Animals that are too squishy to live on land can survive in the ocean because they are supported by the water.

▼ *The sea anemone's tentacles enable it to catch prey, such as small fish.*

▲ *A sea cucumber has hundreds of sticky suction-cup feet that it uses to crawl around on the sea bed.*

Sea cucumbers

Sea cucumbers have warty skin and soft spines. When they are scared, they squeeze their muscles and shoot water out of their bodies. Some sea cucumbers even shoot out their **intestines** at predators to scare them off. Then they grow new intestines.

Sea anemones

Jelly-like sea anemones can be as small as 1.25 centimetres, and some as huge as 1.8 metres. Their mouth is in the centre, surrounded by a ring of tentacles. These tentacles feel sticky to touch, and are used to catch and kill prey. At the slightest touch, the tentacles fire a tiny spike into the prey, injecting it with paralyzing poison.

Box jellyfish

Box jellyfish are sometimes called sea wasps. They look like nearly transparent, box-shaped jellyfish, but they are not actually jellyfish at all. One highly **venomous** species is about the size of a basketball. It has long tentacles that drift behind it as it swims. The tentacles are covered in stinging cells that it uses to kill prey, such as shrimp and small fish.

▼ *Box jellyfish have been called the deadliest creature in the animal kingdom. It is thought they may have killed more than 5500 people since 1954.*

Foul fact!

The venom from some box jellyfish can kill a human in less than 4 minutes!

Slimy pond life

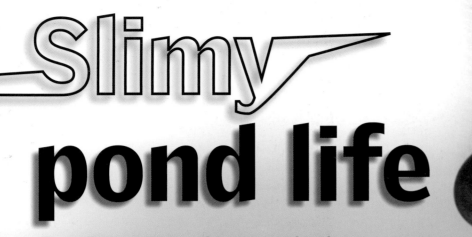

Ponds are seething with slimy life. Hiding behind rocks, slipping through the water and slithering through the weeds are slimy creatures of all shapes and sizes.

▲ *A medicinal leech has three jaws that move backwards and forwards as the leech drinks blood.*

Medicinal leech

Doctors used to think that when people were ill, they would benefit from having some of their blood drained off. To remove the blood, the doctors used leeches. The medicinal leech uses **suction** and slime to attach itself to its prey, or to a person. As it sucks the blood of its prey, the leech dribbles saliva into the wound, making the blood easier to drink.

Foul fact!

The body of a medicinal leech stretches to about 10 times its original size as it fills with blood.

Newts

Newts are found in North America, Europe and Asia. They spend part of their time on land, but they start their lives in fresh water. Newts lay a single egg on plants in ponds or slow-moving streams. They often wrap the egg in a leaf to protect it. The egg hatches into a **larva** with feathery **gills**. Gradually the gills get smaller and the larva grows legs. The young newt, called an eft, is then able to leave the water.

▼ *The poisonous slime of the rough-skinned newt will kill most predators except the common gartersnake, which is **immune** to the poison.*

▲ *Sludge worms live with their heads stuck in the mud and their tails waving in the water.*

Sludge worm

The sludge worm lives in large colonies on the bottom of ponds. It can survive even in very polluted water. The worm eats tiny pieces of food found in the mud that it slurps up.

Soil sliders

Slimy creatures lurk in the soil and on plant leaves. Some use their slimy **faeces** as a disguise, some produce poisonous slime to ward off predators, and some simply use slime to slither along.

Foul fact!

A flatworm gets rid of its faeces through the same opening that it uses to take in food.

▼ *Covered in their own faeces, lily beetle larvae eat up lily leaves, starting at the tips and working their way back to the stem.*

Lily beetle larva

The larva of the scarlet lily beetle is very slimy. It hatches from its egg and covers itself in its own wet, slimy faeces, so that it looks a bit like a bird dropping. This helps to keep it safe from predators. Scarlet lily beetles are serious pests that eat the leaves of lilies and other plants, causing lots of damage.

Flatworms

Flatworms are found in almost every kind of environment – on land, in fresh water and in the sea. There are lots of different types, ranging from tiny worms a few millimetres long to a 27-metre-long monster. Some flatworms, including a group called the flukes, are parasites.

▲ *This striking flatworm lives in the **cloud forests** of Costa Rica.*

Caecilians

Caecilians (pronounced seh-SILL-yens) are tropical amphibians. They look like huge worms, and they burrow in the soil and live in tunnels. Caecilians use their needle-like teeth to catch termites, worms, beetle larvae and other small creatures. They swallow their food whole, without chewing.

◄ *Caecilians produce toxic slime on their skin, which helps to protect them from predators.*

Slimy amphibians

Amphibians spend some of the time on land and some of the time in water. They are able to breathe through their skin, which they need to keep damp and slimy.

▲ The olm is also called the humanfish because its skin is thought to resemble human skin.

Slimy salamanders

Slimy salamanders live in woodland in the United States. They do not have lungs, but take in air through their skin and the lining of their mouth. Slimy salamanders get their name from the slime that oozes from their skin. If you get it on your hands, it will stick like glue.

▼ The sticky slime that slimy salamanders produce makes them a nasty meal for predators.

Olm

The olm lives in caves in parts of Europe. It is albino, which means it has no colour at all in its skin. It is also blind, but has good hearing and a strong sense of smell. The olm preys on crabs, snails and bugs.

Grey foam-nest treefrog

The grey foam-nest treefrog lives mainly in south-east and south-central Africa. It lives in **subtropical** or tropical forests, grassland, shrubland, marshes and even gardens. Foam-nest treefrogs save water in their bodies so that they can live in very dry places. They also produce slime that turns into a waterproof cocoon.

▼ *Pairs of grey foam-nest treefrogs make their foam nest on a branch overhanging rainwater pools. Tadpoles emerge from the eggs, and after about a week drop from the foam into the water below.*

Foul fact!

The grey foam-nest treefrog turns almost white in hot weather. White reflects sunlight, so this helps keep the frog cool.

Slippery skins

Large slimy creatures can be found both on land and in the water. One of the most unusual is the axolotl. It has the unique ability to regrow parts of its body, including its tail and legs, its heart and its brain cells.

▲ *When slime eels are taken out of the water and handled, they drip with sheets of slime.*

Slime eel

The slime eel is a deep-sea eel from the central north Pacific Ocean. It looks similar to the hagfish (see page 27), and has a slitlike mouth and blunt head. The slime eel is a parasite. It burrows into the bodies of halibut and other big fish.

▼ *Unlike most worm lizards, the Mexican worm lizard, or ajolte, has strong front legs and sharp claws for digging.*

Worm lizards

There are more than 150 species of worm lizard. They look a bit like earthworms, but unlike worms their bodies are covered in scales. Worm lizards live underground. Most species do not have legs — they burrow by pushing the soil with their thick, bony skulls. One species, the Florida worm lizard, lives in sandhills and forests in north and central parts of Florida. It grows to about 30 centimetres long and is about as thick as a pencil.

Axolotl

The axolotl lives in only a few freshwater canals near Mexico City. In the wild, it is now an **endangered species**, as its habitat is being destroyed. If its habitat dries up, the axolotl loses its gills and it changes to become a land-living salamander.

▼ *The axolotl has weak eyesight. To find food, it uses its sense of smell and special organs that help it to sense movement.*

Foul fact!

From the 1300s to the 1500s, the Aztec people of Mexico regularly ate axolotls as part of their diet.

23

Slimy bugs

Some slimy creatures cause problems for humans. Millipedes and froghoppers can do terrible damage to crops. Maggots are useful to fishermen, but their parent flies can carry diseases.

▲ Maggots hatch from flies' eggs. The flies lay their eggs on rotten food and on the bodies of dead animals. This provides the maggots with plenty to eat when they hatch.

Maggots

'Maggot' is the name given to fly larvae. Some types of maggot, such as botfly larvae, are parasites. They live under the skin of living animals, causing sores, cuts and even death. This is a real problem in warm, damp climates.

▼ The spotted snake millipede needs to stay damp and slimy. It is most often found in heavy soils, which are less at risk from drying out.

Foul fact!

Millipedes prefer to live in ground that has been covered in manure, or animal faeces.

Snake millipedes

Snake millipedes live in leaf litter, under bark and in moss. They are common in gardens throughout Britain. Snake millipedes use their 200 legs to climb trees, where they graze on green algae. They sometimes find their way into houses, too.

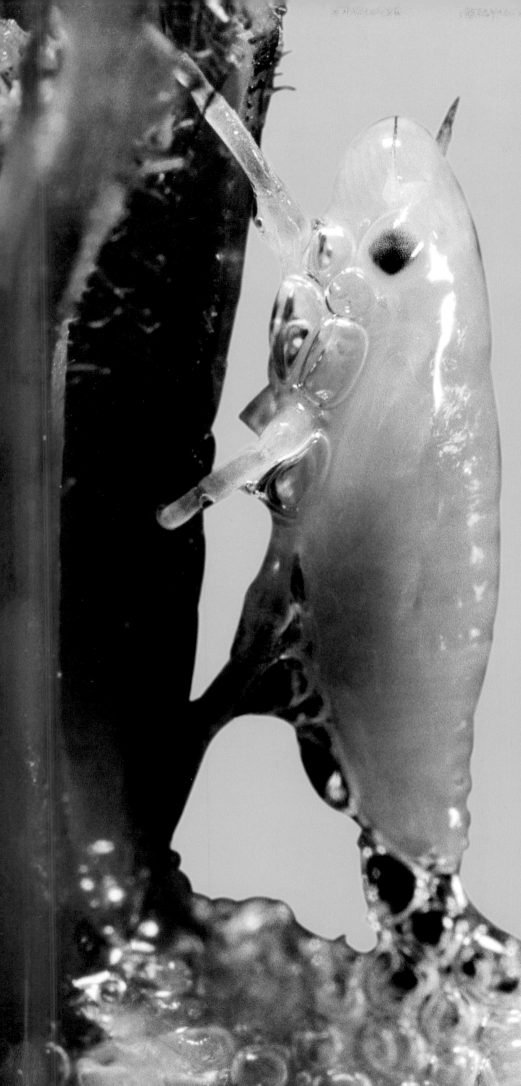

Froghoppers

Froghoppers are small, brown insects that can jump 70 centimetres through the air to reach the next plant. This is an amazing distance for such a tiny creature. Their larvae are known as **nymphs**. For protection, the nymphs develop inside a blob of froth, called cuckoo spit, often seen on grass. The froth hides the nymph from predators, keeps it damp and stops it from getting too hot or cold.

◄ *A froghopper nymph, or spittlebug, creates its protective froth by blowing air into a fluid excreted from its **anus**.*

Super slimers

Of all the slimy animals in the world, the hagfish must be one of the slimiest. Another weird slimer is slime mould, which sometimes behaves like an animal and sometimes like a plant.

▼ *The common mudpuppy has a small range in parts of Canada and the United States. It has moist, slimy skin.*

▲ *Many slime moulds are brightly coloured. They have names such as the dog's vomit slime mould and the scrambled-egg slime mould.*

Slime moulds

Slime moulds are very strange. For part of its life a slime mould looks like a collection of tiny mushrooms or a crusty deposit on a rotting log. When it is reproducing, it turns into a slimy jelly and can creep around.

Common mudpuppy

The common mudpuppy is an amphibian. Most young amphibians lose their gills as they grow and become adults, but the common mudpuppy is different. It keeps it gills and spends its whole life underwater. It prefers to live in shallow lakes or slow-moving streams with rocks to hide under. It eats snails, larvae, worms, small fish and crayfish.

Hagfish

If caught by a predator and held by the tail, hagfish try to escape by secreting quantities of slime from their skin and glands. Hagfish slime includes strong fibres up to 12 centimetres long, similar to spider silk. The fibres are unusual in that they never get tangled. Researchers are trying to find ways of using the fibres to help accident victims and surgery patients, by helping to stop bleeding.

Foul fact!

An adult hagfish can change a bucket of water into slime in a few minutes.

▼ *A hagfish produces slime if it is alarmed or disturbed. It may also use slime to deter predators from taking the eggs in its nest.*

Make it!

Make your own bowl of slithery cornflour slime, and have a slimy sliders party. Imagine you are one of the amazing slippery animals you have seen in this book.

You will need:

1 cup
1 packet of cornflour
Water – $\frac{1}{4}$ cup
Mixing bowl
Spoon
Washing-up bowl
Glitter
Beads

1 Fill a cup with cornflour and tip it into a mixing bowl. Then measure out $\frac{1}{4}$ cup of water.

2 Slowly add the water to the cornflour, stirring all the time.

3 When the cornflour and water have mixed together smoothly and there is no dry cornflour left on the sides of the bowl, tip the slimy mixture into a washing-up bowl.

4 You can add things to the slime to make it even more fun, such as glitter or beads or green food colouring. Always make sure there is an adult to help you.

5 Plunge your hands into the slime and feel it change from hard and thick to soft and runny — and back again!

Glossary

Algae

Certain types of plants that grow in or near water. They do not have ordinary leaves or roots.

Allergy

Someone who has an allergy is sensitive to certain things, such as pollen or animal hair. Allergic reactions may make a person sneeze or break out in an itchy rash.

Amphibian

Creatures that live on land and in water, such as frogs and newts.

Anus

The hole in the body from which faeces are pushed out.

Calcium

Bones, teeth and shells are made of calcium, which is a natural material. Calcium is essential for the normal growth and development of most animals and plants.

Camouflage

An animal that is camouflaged is difficult to spot because its patterns or colours blend with the background.

Cells

Every living thing is made up of many tiny cells. Skin is made up of skin cells, for example.

Cellulose

All plant tissues and fibres are made of cellulose, a material that does not dissolve in water. Cellulose is used to make paper, cellophane, fabrics and even explosives.

Cloud forests

In cloud forests, mist or clouds are found at very low levels. This blocks a lot of the direct sunlight, and the air is very damp. The mist turns into water droplets on the leaves, and these drip to the ground.

Cocoon

A cocoon is a silky pouch spun by the larvae of many insects, such as silkworms and caterpillars. It covers the larva and keeps it safe as it develops into an adult.

Endangered species

An endangered species is in danger of dying out or becoming extinct.

Faeces

Waste matter that passes out from an animal's anus as droppings.

Fungi

The group of plants that contains yeasts, moulds and mushrooms.

Gastropod

Gastropods include snails and slugs that live on land, water snails and sea slugs. They move by sliding along on their rubbery foot. Most gastropods live in the sea or in rivers and ponds.

Gills

The organs that help animals that live in water to breathe. The gills take oxygen from the water.

Glands

Organs that produce a natural substance for use in the body. Salivary glands produce saliva, for example.

Immune

To be protected from, or not affected by, something, such as a disease or poison.

Intestines

Intestines join the stomach and the anus, and help a creature's body to digest food.

Larva

The newly hatched stage of certain creatures, such as butterflies and ladybirds. Larvae change to become quite different-looking creatures as adults.

Leaf litter

Dead plant material made from decaying leaves, twigs and bark.

Lichen

A type of dry-looking fungus with many tiny branches. Lichen grows on rocks and trees.

Mucus

A slimy substance secreted by the body.

Nymph

Nymphs are the larval stage of some animals. They change into an adult form.

Parasite

An organism that lives on or inside another organism, called a host. The parasite feeds off the host.

Phytoplankton

Tiny, free-floating water plants.

Predator

A creature that hunts and kills other animals for food.

Prey

An animal that is hunted by another animal.

Protein

A food group needed for growth and the repair of injuries.

Radula

A radula is a mollusc's flexible tongue. It has horny teeth, used for scraping up food.

Saliva

The liquid produced in the mouth to keep it wet and healthy.

Secrete

To produce substances from cells in the body. Sweat is secreted through the skin.

Species

A group of animals who share characteristics. Animals of the same species can breed with each other.

Spittle

Saliva that has been spat out.

Subtropical

The regions next to the tropics are called subtropical.

Suction

Gripping on to something by sucking. Some animals have suction cups on their feet or legs that help them to grip.

Tentacle

Tentacles are the long, flexible parts of certain animals, such as jellyfish. They are used for feeling and moving.

Tropical

Tropical relates to the tropics – the area on either side of the equator. The tropics are usually hot and damp.

Venomous

A venomous creature uses poison tp paralyze or kill its prey.

Index